CONTENTS

CHAPTER 1 .... **3**
   A BILLION ATTEMPTS 3

CHAPTER 2 .... **19**
   FROM ADVERSITY TO GREATNESS 19

CHAPTER 3 .... **28**
   INTEGRATING THE HIDDEN STRENGTH OF YOUR DARK SIDE 28

CHAPTER 4 .... **42**
   UNLOCKING YOURSELF 42

Chapter 5 .... **47**
   CREATING YOUR OPPORTUNITIES 47

CHAPTER 6 .... **51**
   THE WARRIOR WITHIN 51

CHAPTER 7 .... **56**
   YOUR THOUGHTS CREATES YOUR LIFE 56

CHAPTER 8 .... **59**
   HEARTFULNESS - DISCOVERING YOURSELF 59

Chapter 9 .... **69**
   The View 69

Dedication

This book is a dedication to my dad and mom; I am who I am because of you and thank you for all the unconditional love and support. To my brother who has stood by like a rock and won all the challenges that have come his way – Vishnu, you inspire me and many more. To my wife for being patient with me through this journey. To my friends, for their constant positive nudge in the right direction.

And

To John – Thank you!

"Your Heart is your Laboratory

You are the scientist &

You are the Judge"

- Chariji

CHAPTER 1

A BILLION ATTEMPTS

The American dream was my parent's or my society's golden achievement. Me coming to the united states was something that I had not dreamt about. Being a mediocre student -I always envied the brighter ones that made things look so simple that I was still compared to their achievements. It was a rat race out there and more than anything, a pursuit to a system that has a never-ending cycle.

I finished my engineering and made my parents proud. Well, I did not want to take engineering; I am not going to say that it was a dream come true, usually in India, if you are a male child you need to finish an engineering degree and if you are a female child you need to be a doctor or a housewife mostly. These were society's stereotypes, and if you did not do this, they (society) would consider you a failure. Another engineer for in the land of a million engineers but I proudly pat myself on my back that I did to get dragged into the web of doing I.T. but rather fascinated with machines and took Mechanical Engineering. I thought I was done, no more books, no more exams – I had by then gotten selected in a company and had started working. Work was mundane, and I did not enjoy it, and I wanted to join my dad in his work line. I never did want to do anything more to do with studies but what do you know that dream of never touching a book again was shattered. Here comes a family member and says, "oh, my daughter is in the USA," and your son also must try it and go. Well, Walla, now our dinner table conversations went into you should try to go and do your masters. It kept working on the back of my mind; on the one hand, I did not have the heart to leave everything that I love and on the other hand, the freedom and multiple opportunities out there to explore. I decide to give it go and decide to give TOEFL a go and surprisingly scored well (beyond my own expectation), and then GRE came by and my spirits came crashing down. Damn! I thought I could get through GRE the same I did TOEFL. Nevertheless, I finally get an admit and head towards the United States of America.

Now I myself never imagined that I would get myself this far, but I did. Now the reality of moving to the united states kicks in. Still, one big thing remained "the U.S. visa interview" – it's like the holy grail of all interviews and examination.

Once my date was scheduled for the interview, the preparations started happening. Firstly I had to secure the bank loan that needs to be funded for my education – this was already a burden on me as I did not want my parents to go through all the hardship of paying the loans. In due course of time, the loan got approved, and the value seemed to be a daunting task for me to pay off, but with an iron will, I was hopeful that I could. As the interview date got closer, the tensions started rising. I was advised to look into all the possible questions that the Visa officer at the consular officer might ask.

I wondered to myself that I am applying for a simple student visa and why there is so much fanfare. I later learned that there is an entire business module surrounding the interview process – they coach you on how to answer the questions, what documents to take, how to fill out the forms and even to tell us what food items to take while traveling to the USA and what not to take. To my astonishment, these centers are more difficult to get an appointment rather than getting a university admission. For a simpleton brain like mine, I wondered why this process was so exhausting mentally for everyone. Was this what they call the golden object syndrome?

These are based on the events and programs that have been imbibed in us as a child. The age of 0-7 is a crucial time in our lives. The events around us, the unconscious and conscious things we do and listen to, and our parents' behavioral patterns are deeply coded into our brains. As adults, we bring out the actions subconsciously. It's like your brain was plugged into a download mode for the first seven years of your life. Past that phase, we continue to build on that platform to become who we are today. For us to make the changes in our lives, we need to reprogram our unconscious brain and that's the secret friends, to achieve the changes we need to achieve and the programs that were previously instilled in me was fear of failure and the shame that I would go through if I did not the set goals.

Finally, the visa interview date arrived. I travel from Bangalore to Chennai; all prepared to face the ultimate interview of a lifetime. I got through the long wait and it was my turn next in line to be interviewed. This was the defining moment of what all the hype was in the last few months. It was like standing before GOD and waiting for the verdict to be sentenced to go to heaven or hell. The interview starts. The officer asks me a couple of questions and asks for some specific documents, and I hand that over to him. He asked me why I choose this University to go to – now I had two answers in my head. One was that out of the four universities I had applied to; this was the best one. Two was to tell the officer that this University was the best in the engineering stream I was choosing. I choose the initial answer. The officer was typing something on his computer as I was giving him the responses. He never made eye contact except when he asked me something. I was probably there for about 5-7 mins, but it seemed like an eternity to me.

Finally, the officer told me that my visa application was approved and that I can expect my stamped passport to come back in a week. I thank the officer, leave the interview hall, and walk back towards the exit with many emotions running inside me. Should I be excited that I got approved and will be going to the united states or a sudden feeling of sadness that I will be leaving everything near and dear to me – my parents, brother, home, bed, food, and my motherland? I walk out with mixed feelings but with a smile on my face. My dad greets me outside the consulate and asks me what happened from a distance, and I gave him a thumbs up from a distance, and he was relieved more than me that I had been approved. Now I put myself in my parents' shoes the sacrifice and pain that they must go through to educate their children and make them into the person they are today for their Kids well being and partially to satisfy the wagging tongues of the society and to prove them that yes we have done our duty and have sent my son abroad for higher studies. This was somewhat of a social ego, but Heart of Heart, even to this date, I knew that the day I boarded the flight to the united states, was the toughest day of my life. I could not bear to see the tears in my parent's eyes. There was no excitement that I was flying to a completely new country but leaving my parents and bidding them goodbye has been the most difficult part of my life.

Once the visa had been approved, all of a sudden, I was this unnoticed kid in the neighborhood and became everyone's attention for the next few weeks – only because I had been approved for this visa. Here I am, the golden boy now for some people with envy and others with genuine admiration. For a minute, I thought that all the people around me felt that I could achieve this and I was the one who did not believe in myself.

Time starts ticking and I was looking at all the messages coming in, friends and relatives visiting to bid farewell to me. It was a very nostalgic feeling, and I thought to myself, why is going to the united states such a big deal? I was reading the newspaper the next day. I read this story where a boy had committed suicide because his visa was not approved and was shamed by his relatives for not having the approval. I was shocked. Is the united states the land of the American dream and is the U.S. dollar the ultimate goal? I became quite inquisitive to see if the grass was really "greener" on the other side.

India has the world's largest engineering colleges pool and every year they produce them in the thousands. I use the word producing rather than graduating for a reason. That's awesome, is it not – but does India have enough jobs to hire all these candidates – NOPE. My dad said that it was an achievement in his younger days if someone would do their graduation and it was a big deal. When marriage was settled with these engineers and doctors, it was a social status for the families. This practice is there even to this date. The only difference is the bar has risen that the couple needs to be postgraduates, preferably from the united states. Damn, I was shocked that one country could play into the minds of so many middle and upper-middle-class families in India.

Day to flyout draws closer, and I start congratulatory calls from people I have never met in my life; this is the USA's power, I thought – a piece of paper called a visa had made me from a regular individual to a superstar. I am now looking forward to this American dream and started getting a bit excited. I thought I had achieved the biggest award of getting a US VISA.

Come the day; I admire the "green" dollar in my hand after converting all the Indian rupees I had saved up. The day to depart arrived, and I felt weird about how to bid goodbye to my ailing grandmother. She was not aware that I was flying away to a faraway land and as I left the house, I told her that I was leaving for a short tour and will be back in a couple of days. I was teary-eyed, and my heart sank when she held my hand and said, take care of yourself and take care of dad. I had a hunch she figured out that I was leaving for the united states. I held her hand for one last time and bid goodbye, and little did I know that was the last time I would be seeing her in person alive.

Each one of us has so many emotions and values built inside of us. We continue to strive every day to be a better person; the actions we commit, emotions that we show and words that we speak are all programmed into our subconscious mind by our surroundings. Emotional pain is an example of an individual's life. For me, it was heartbreaking when I left home for the United States.

Broadly all of them fall under four major categories as Egocentric, Ethnocentric, World Centric and Spirit centric. Nothing in the below is either good or bad; it's just each person's programming and learnings they have had in the lifetime.

Egocentric	Ethnocentric	World Centric	Spirit Centric
Values Level 1	Values Level 4	Values Level 6	Values Level 7
Values Level 2	Values Level 5		Values Level 8
Values Level 3			

When we talk about *Egocentric individuals* – they are selfish, and they care only about themselves and their needs first. They are set on their ways of thinking and will not budge from their views.

Ethnocentric Individuals: Are individuals that view the world in their eyes in comparison to the values and standards, tribal or their own sets and beliefs

worldcentric Individuals: Individuals who care about the world, society and human connection

Spirit Centric: individuals who have realized the heart's power and the unconscious mind are in sync.

As per author John Qreshi, he explains these values as consciousness levels.

VALUES LEVEL 1: Instinct Survival Mode

Individuals at this level are instinct-driven; their actions are mainly driven for day to day survival. E.g., food, shelter, pleasure, protection etc.

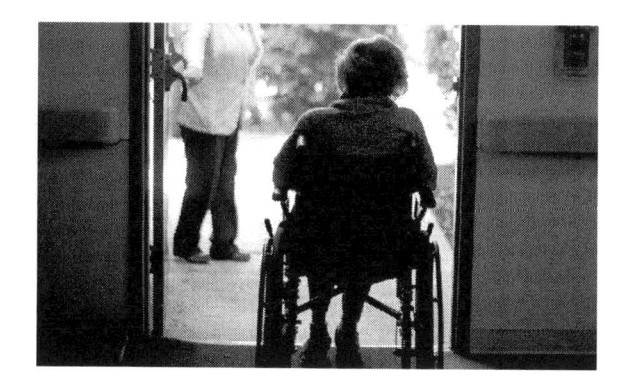

Value Level 2: Tribal Order

Individuals of this value level are completely focused on their safety. They live in the illusion that if they follow certain rituals or taboos or carry their talisman around, they would be rewarded with safety or vice versa. They believe by following certain superstitious beliefs; they would be rewarded. It can vary from a tribe carrying out certain rituals according to their Folkfore to please the Gods to a person carrying a Talisman for good luck.

Ref: https://www.legendsofamerica.com/na-ceremonies/

Values Level 3: Power of God

Individuals in this value level crave power, usually are very egocentric, impulsive and would not like to bow down to others. The primary goal is to reach higher standards, even if it means exploiting people on their way up. They feel they are unique to differentiate themselves from others around them. People in this value level can be associated with dominant power-hungry people with a lack of empathy.

Ref:https://www.thoughtco.com/the-conquistadors-2136575

Values Level 4: Order and the absolute

At this level, the individuals are part of a group that follows a certain set of rigid principles with strict adherence and enforcement. The structure usually is very authoritative and requires the followers to maintain the traditions and rules set by them. Follow the rules or face the consequences is what this value level follows.

Values Level 5: the Suceeder

People at this value level aim to reach their goals and strive for success. They could take various means of analyzing and strategizing their ideas to reach their respective goals. They're very innovative and find the most beneficial method to win their game.

VALUES LEVEL 6: SOCIALLY GREEN CONSCIOUS

At this level, individuals are driven by compassion and have a sense of unity. They believe in oneness and are against the hierarchal way of living. Individuals at this level explore their inner self and Avoid conflict. They are compassionate, soft-spoken, good at social interactions and have deep personal relations.

VALUES LEVEL 7: INTEGRATED / FLEX-FLOW

Individuals of this level are similar to those of level 6 tey to have a sensitive, caring nature and have close ties to human spiritual values; they believe in a community rather than a hierarchical system. There is a lack of fear of staying alive at this value level having the shelter of predators of disapproval of status and God. They are expressive and free natured.

VALUES LEVEL 8: <u>AN AWAKENED SOUL</u>

At this level, individuals are not only connected to other people, but everything around them as well. They are sensitive to harmonic and mystical forces.

As I continue to let my mind wander in my value level and deep thoughts, I leave for the airport and board the plane with a heavy heart. As the plane climbs in altitude, I closed my eyes, and my heart was torn to pieces. Is this dream worth sacrificing all the love, warmth and closeness to the family that you will miss and as the feeling sunk in took out my wallet to put on the front porch and pulled out a dollar bill and thought maybe the grass is greener on the other side - and boy was I surprised!!!

"one day? Or day one?

— you decide

CHAPTER 2

FROM ADVERSITY TO GREATNESS

I was fast asleep when the flight attendant wakes me up for dinner. I get up thinking about who is waking me up in the middle of the night. Then the reality hits me that I'm on a flight and I'm on the way to the United States of America. I sat up a little bit excited. Food excites me a lot, and I was looking forward to it actually, and I was given the menu and choices when I had to choose between chicken and beef. I tell the flight attendant, and we may have a problem here, and I am completely vegetarian. I do not eat beef or chicken, so is there something I could eat that is Meat-free? The answer was a complete astounding NO, and I could eat only the sides I had to give up on my main course. I was a little disappointed when this happened because I was really looking forward to the food. I was like, damn is this going to be the struggle that I'm going to have to go through in the United States to look for vegetarian food. I enjoyed the movies on the flight and my first pitstop was at London Heathrow airport. This is the first time I'm getting out of the country, and I was pretty nervous about being around people from other countries. I was just a naïve Indian kid with a backpack running from pillar to post, not knowing where to go. I was shying away from trying to reach out to anyone out there as I thought people would look at me that I am an Indian, I am brown-skinned and that would lead to racism.I was scared even to go and look at somebody - and I am talking to them. I did not know how to make a phone call; I had limited currency with me, and I did not know if I would be ripped off or will somebody really help me out. I was looking for a phone booth to call my cousin who lives in London to tell her to make a call to my dad and tell him that I've safely made it halfway through. I was not able to get a hold of her left a voicemail. For God's sake, I don't even know what to voicemail why I said that point. I know that my parents would be anxious; they would not be sleeping, waiting to hear from me, and trying my best to communicate. Luckily for me, my cousin got the voicemail, and she informed my dad that I had made it to London. No, the exciting part of the journey begins I bought the flight to land in the Chicago United States. This is the American dream that I've been waiting for, or for lack of better terms, the entire family's been waiting for. No, my first experience started when the flight got Delayed and took about two hours Circling me there. My flight was circling midair before it lands two hours later. What This did to me was to miss my flight to Dallas Fort Worth. This was a nightmare for me. I had no clue as to what needs to be done. I've missed my flight, and I did not know who I would ask for help. I asked the gentleman to help me make a phone call to my friend who expects to pick me up from the airport at Dallas-Fort Worth he straight up refused. I felt small in front of this American, and in my mind, I felt humiliated that he did not offer to help me make a phone call. In my mind, I was painting a picture of how I'm going to be treated in the United States. Would somebody not help me out by just making a phone call as I was new to the country and all I needed was to make one phone call to inform my friend that I'm going to be late. But to my surprise, I was helped by the friendly staff audio hurry airport and guided me to the right place to board the next flight outbound towards Dallas. I finish customs pass through all the formalities and board my flight towards Dallas, Texas. I land pretty late at the Dallas international airport, and my friend was there to pick me up along with his uncle. I greeted him and exchanged pleasantries and was pretty excited to finally reached my destination. My friend immediately tells me that my parents had called him and were pretty worried that I had and landed on the flight I was supposed to land and to add to the anxiety, my friend informed my mom that the flight from Heathrow to Chicago was not able to land due to weather conditions and was circling midair and this added to the anxiety. We finally get into the car, and I called my parents. They were so excited to hear my voice, and I could hear that the entire experience has been overwhelming for my parents and I could sense the crying in their voice. They were finally relieved that the ordeal of me flying from India to the United States was over.

Finally, I reach the University of Texas at Arlington. We offload our bags and go up the stairs into my apartment. I was greeted by a few friendly faces who asked me about where I am from, what I do which course and said I was in good hands. I was tired of this long journey and wanted to rest. I was excited that I could go out and check out our new campus. I have not seen a carpet before, and there was no bed ready for me. My friend had purchased a comforter for me and handed it over to me. I spread it out on the carpet, and I lay down, and I think to myself, this is my first day in the United States and I'm already sleeping on the floor. I remembered my bed and the cozy feeling and closed my eyes and went off into a deep sleep and woke up pretty late in the morning the next day. Nobody was in the apartment, and I walk around the two levels, and I could not find my friend. I did not have a cell phone yet and had no idea how to communicate. I was hungry and had to go and look for some food. I did not know what to eat. I'm struggling here on the first day that I've landed in the United States, and I was dying to know what was in store for me in the coming few months. The dream of the grass being greener on the other side I am looking at it trying to find grass to eat.

I started getting along with my roommates and slowly got that class has started. I was really excited with the way the curriculum was going on, and I had my challenges. I could now sleep whenever I wanted and only had a few classed to attend per week, which was a big change from the universities back home. Now the next big challenge was to get a job on campus. Me being an international student would let me work only for 20 hours on campus. I tried to get my seniors' help to guide me on what job I could take up and what would help me out. To my astonishment, I found out that getting an on-campus job was the most difficult part. I was like, here we go again; what am I going to do? Am I going to rely on my dad to keep sending me funds for my day-to-day expenses or am I going to bother sack up and try to find a job to take care of my monthly expenses? Now I get introduced to the new Term called Social Security. Apparently, I could not be hired without having a number. So I said out in the pursuit of trying to find a job so that they could give me an offer letter and I could apply at the Social Security office to get a Social Security number. I've never felt so deflated in my life where I could not find a single job for about six months; that was the level of competition at the University.

Somehow, after all the struggles, I ended up getting a job at Chick-fil-A at the university and a couple of days into my training. On the job, the manager asked me to go upfront and clean the tables. I was furious that he would give me such a job because this was such a menial job back in India. It was meant for only the uneducated and less privileged people. Him asking me to do that job infuriated me. Still, I had no choice. I took the tub and the sponge and cleaned the table. The couple sitting in front of the table happily talked and thanked me for cleaning the table and placed a two dollar tip on the table for me. I had tears rolling down my eyes; how could I - being a master's student be asked to clean tables? In the evening, I call my dad and tell him the incident as to what happened at Chick-fil-A that morning. I expected him to be as furious as me and tell me to pack my bags up and come back to India. I did not have to go through the struggle. Instead, he told me that it was a good experience and I had learned an excellent lesson to respect all jobs, all people and the value of money. On that day, something changed inside of me. I was a completely different person after that; I started seeing things in a different light. I learn to stand on my feet that day and respect every person for who he is and respect every job that any individual does.

My studies and struggles continue at the University. Still, I learn to live with this and am getting settled in. Now, something interesting happens, and I was shocked. We have traveled far, and I thought that all Indians would be together here and live happily. Little did I sense that there were so much politics among the students living there.

After six months, the seniors graduated and handed over the apartment's lease to me. At that point, I was looking for new roommates. One new student turns up, and he wanted temporary accommodation for a few days before finding a suitable apartment – I was OK to help and also offered for him to be my roommate. He politely declined to stay and stated that he was a strict vegetarian and would prefer to live in an apartment where there is no non-veg being cooked in the kitchen. Even though I thought that was a bullshit reason, I respected his decision as I had been around people who have had reservations. I had recently converted to being a vegetarian for just lifestyle changes. Now I referred him to a room where I thought he would be comfortable. He comes back later that evening and tells me that he could not live in that apartment as he would not be comfortable; I asked him why and the reason he gave shocked me. He said that even though they speak the same language, they are from a different cast and I am from a different cast and would not get along. I was flabbergasted and asked him to pack his bags and leave my apartment to find different temporary accommodation. Here we are thousands of miles away from our country and we still discriminate within our own people.

I learn in due course of time it hurts me to say that we are the most racist people in the world; we discriminate based on religion, based on the job, based on money and wealth, based on what you drive, based on who you get married to, based on what bank balance you have, based on what you wear, who you pray to, who you talk to, what you practice, your ideologies and you name it and we will discriminate. Suddenly the hunter is being hunted and we turn crying fox when we feel discriminated against. I have been guilty of it, and I have done this myself at certain instances in my life as well. We see what we are and those are our shadows. We need to look at ourselves in the mirror and work on ourselves before we blame anyone else.

"Everything that irritates us about others can lead us to a better understanding of ourselves"

– Carl Jung

CHAPTER 3

INTEGRATING THE HIDDEN STRENGTH OF YOUR DARK SIDE

Our shadows are always following us, during the day and the night. This shadow is not the visible shadow but the shadows that have been created within us due to our past impressions. One of our biggest strengths as human beings is we are given the power to identify our very own faults. We can reflect on our habits, our doings, our anger, our resentment, our revenge, our struggles, and our hurts. All of these form the shadows within us and our unconscious mind is always tapping into this and makes us react to who we are. We draw our actions based on our shadows – and if we do not address our negative traits, it can lead to a lot of hurt and wrongful decisions in life. We must first have the consciousness to accept that we have these negative traits; only if we detect a shadow we can work on it.

I was very engrossed watching youtube videos where one after another, the bot kept suggesting videos of people confronting drunk people – some were funny, and some were very violent. For a moment, I was thinking to myself as to why these videos keep coming and why it spikes my interest. I was getting enraged with Driving under the influence of alcohol – the unwanted fights they would pick up and physical assault. It angered me to the point that I was getting frustrated with small things at home. Then the most interesting things happened within a couple of weeks of the video viewing – I was out with my wife at a restaurant along with a few friends. It was already pretty late at night and after bidding goodbye to my friends, we walked up to my car, and we sat inside it. From nowhere, this guy shows up and pulls on the door handle to open; luckily, it was locked. I ask my wife to sit in the car, and I step out.

I am not someone who likes conflicts, usually do not get involved and try to be at a distance – on the contrary, my personality and my appearance paints a very different picture to the other person. As I step out of the car – this guy notices a six-foot, 230 lb standing in front of him and it was not at all my intention to engage in conversation, let alone threaten him. I politely ask him to step aside from my car so that I can back up and leave. He would not and starts abusing me and even threatens to flip the car upside down – who does he think he is? The HULK. I was very red and upset and asking him to move, and my wife was yelling from inside the car for me to get in so that it does not get into a big fight. At this very moment, I realize to myself – did I see all these videos and that constantly thinking about overly drunk people and their antics attract this very moment towards me? Well! I thought to myself – I was looking to attract so many better things in life and attract this lunatic towards me? I laughed a little, and I calmed down. I walked up to the office in the front of the restaurant and explained the situation, and he was more than happy to help me out by taking this guy away from my car.

I think to myself, why did I bring this upon me – I had never encountered these scenarios in the past. Was this my own Shadow reflecting? I drove away from that scene and reached home. Had I not known about these teachings from John- I could have reacted very differently to this situation.

The most negative experiences we have had in our lives are in our unconscious mind; it's a psychological scar. These scars turn in shadows, and they stimulate harmful recollections. Like people in every case, we unwittingly hold counting on those shadows to shield ourselves from experiencing similar negative situations in our lives. These scars do not leave us and keep coming back to unconsciously protect ourselves and sometimes gives out our alternative negative characteristics. All of these are programmed in our minds from the ages of 0-7, the environment around us, and family and friends' behavior. As we grow older, we accumulate more of these shadows.

In physiological terms, our shadow insinuates all that we cannot discover in ourselves. The shadow is the "blurred side" of our character. It includes essentially simple, negative sentiments and main forces like indignation, resentment, insatiability, conceit, and the quest for power.

The Risk of Ignoring Your Shadow: Our ancestors understood the need to honor all of the psyche parts. For them, these parts were worshipped as gods and goddesses. A god or goddess you ignored became the one who you angered and destroyed you. When we look in the mirror, our personal shadow is our very own qualities that we have disowned and despise in others. We try to let go of this shadow and when we encounter these shadows in others, it angers us. We need to understand that these are our own mental stigma, issues and qualities that need to be worked on. We need to take personal learnings from all the actions we do and encounter.

Effects of Repressing your Shadow: Each person has a shadow side. The greater part of our unconscious mind puts forth an admirable attempt to shield our mental self-portrait from anything unflattering or new. So it's frequently simpler for us to watch another person's shadow before recognizing our own shadow or pessimistic conduct. In any case, whatever characteristics we deny in ourselves, we will likewise discover in others. In psychology, this is called projection. We project onto others anything we bury within us. If, for example, you get irritated when someone is rude to you, there is a good chance you haven't owned your own rudeness. Any part we disown within us eventually turns against us. Our personal shadow represents a collection of these disowned parts. Problems happen because our shadow side operates on its own, without our full awareness. Remaining unconscious of our shadow self often hurts our relationships with our spouses, family, and friends. It impacts our professional relationships and leadership abilities. We do things we would not voluntarily do and later regret. We say things we would not say. Our facial reactions express emotions we do not consciously feel. We get triggered by someone else's actions because we deny that behavior in ourselves deep down.

Working On Our Shadows: It is believed that our shadow side is a reflection of our power, honesty and passion. If we want to feel whole and balanced and to continue growing and truly heal, we must begin by making friends with our negative side. The first step in shadow work is to become aware of ongoing patterns in your life. Do you consistently encounter the same problems or experience recurring feelings? These patterns can help to highlight your shadow.

Common shadow beliefs include:

- I am not good enough.

- I am not capable of experiencing love.
- I am flawed.
- My feelings are not valid.
- I must take care of everyone around me.
- Why can't I just be normal?

Exploring your shadow can lead to greater authenticity, creativity, energy, and personal clarity and happiness. Shadow work can bring you inner strength and a greater sense of balance, making you better equipped to take on life's challenges. We can start embracing our shadow side by becoming more consciously aware of our thoughts and interactions with others. By becoming more mindful of our thoughts, we can learn to simply observe and not react to situations that previously triggered negative behavior or the shadow aspects of ourselves.

A good way to practice being more mindful is to simply:

a. Treat your thoughts as if they are clouds floating by in the sky. Let them come and go but do not judge or try to fight them. Simply accept and appreciate them for what they are.

b. Facing our shadow is rewarding yet challenging life-long work. A big part of healing and finding more peace is doing shadow work. Once you become aware of how your shadow beliefs are holding you back from living your fullest life, you can consciously change your behavior and, in doing so, change your life.

Our shadows are something that travels along with us every day. Our mind has the power to manifest our actions. Some of the laws of nature are in the play when we can talk about the law of attraction and manifestation. When we encounter a situation like that, there are learnings for us to take from these events.

Sources:

A Definitive Guide to Jungian Shadow Work: How to Get to Know and Integrate Your Dark Side" Scott Jeffrey

A Little Book on the Human Shadow Robert Bly

The Mindbody Prescription: Healing the Body, Healing the Pain John E. Sarno M.D.

Law of compensation:

Every action we take has an equal and opposite reaction, says Newton's third law - We need to send out to nature for it to give something back to us. Life is action, and we must find work and interests of some sort to prevent mental and physical decay; there is a law of compensation running through life and the universe and cannot be avoided.

To experience success, we must strive to work hard and accomplish. To receive the riches of the world, we must give our best in our thoughts and actions. Give the best form of you to the world and the best will come back to you - what you think you become. You put negative thoughts in your mind. It results in negative actions. Put in the positive thought and witness the magic happen. The entire world will conspire to give you the best of everything - this is where the law of attraction operates, not by sitting still.

The principle of fair deal runs through all life in the universe; if an artist conceives a picture - if his content remains in his mind, should he get paid for his creativity? Would it be right if payment was made to him for a picture that existed only in his imagination? As he is not rendered any service to others, he's not given any value for money. He puts his picture on a canvas and brings joy to others - payment for his services is made. Life demands fair exchange; if we are to receive - we must give; if we give, we will receive. Underhand dealing and taking advantage of other people's weaknesses does not lead to success. There are plenty of men equipped in life - brainy, resourceful and capable and not lacking in courage. Still, they have not succeeded because they are not straightforward. They may be clever and do well at first interviews, but they can never keep their clients because they failed to give honest service in exchange for honest money.

This world is crying out for honest, straightforward and sincere business people, politicians' preachers and teachers. It beckons for men and women of integrity, men and women who live their lives according to a principle instead of mere opportunists. For men and women who love honor and truth, the world wants people who will give their very best and is willing to pour out their treasures. Principle and sincerity are needed today more than ever, people who can be trusted. The world can rely on no great successes or ever can be possible without the quality of sincerity; no great accomplishment was ever won except by those whose honor and principle were true.

Look at the lives of the majority of truly great and successful people, and you will find sincerity of purpose, a giving of their very best service to the world. The extent of their sincerity is the measure of their greatness. You may not want greatness; your ideas of success may be simply an increase of salary, which is a moderate fortune or well-paid job in your calling or profession to be a great author or politician or poet or philosopher or leader of men or a person great enough in character to carve your name in the history of your time.

It may not spike your interest to the slightest degree or on the other hand, they may, but whatever your ambition maybe, you and only you can realize it. If you are dedicated to winning success of any kind, You must be sincere. You must give your very best. You must somehow find an expression for what it is this within you. You come into conscious realization of the powers you possess.

You have more to express; therefore, your best will constantly be getting better. The consequences that you will be rewarded with will be greater - in other words, as you evolve within, as you build up in a manner unseen, propel your will, your inner self to achieve and manifest - in your life, success and prosperity will be attracted to you. All of this depends on you giving freely; if you give grudgingly, you will receive a limited reward; if you give completely and freely of the very best within, you will reap a rich and plentiful harvest. Always give the best that is within you; give your best thoughts hold nothing back.

Give your most dedicated service and do not spare yourself - for all the cosmic forces are yours. Give to the utmost of all - the powers, the forces, the emotions and the inspirations within you to discover. The universe is not run by chance; everything is according to law, the law of compensation is immutable and it can never be evaded; these are scientific facts.

We hold our destinies and lives in our own hands; we can give our best to the world in every aspect, in love and in devotion, In honesty and faithfulness, In inspiration and beauty, the best in all that we do and the universe will conspire for you and bring back the highest good and the greatest of joy. On the other hand, if we choose to give to the world and the people around us hate, deceit and grabbing an advantage by unethical means. We are destined to attract a harvest of troubles, disappointment, unhappiness and failure.

You are entering into the fullness and glory of the vast powers of your subliminal mind and controlling an ever-growing stream of creative thoughts. These inward forces are being translated into action. That action can only be better service, better work, higher accomplishment and more abundant success than you have ever known before. You now live in a more conscious present and press onto still more perfect future mistakes, and shortcomings of the past will have no more control over you.

In your hands are the keys that open up the way to all the freedom and accomplishment. From now on, the new and wonderful life within you will swell up with ever-increasing power and find expression, better work and tasks more perfectly performed. Service more generously, given complete self-control, leave the past and its perceived failures. Today is yours, and the future will be according as you build today. Use the following affirmation I give to the world the best. We do not have to run after success and fortune; rather, they kneel at my feet and pay me respect.

Everything I need is mine, and all that I desire comes to me by the operation of natural law. I realize now that I am one with and for my part of the infinite mind. I require Peace of Mind and that will help the body achieve friends, love, prosperity success. these are all mine they race to assist in my eternal joy I am a magnet I tried to myself only the highest good I am attuned only to the highest vibration of health success accomplishment and happiness the lower vibrations of disease failure want and unhappiness can find no echo in my mind no manifestation in my life I am in my inner higher better self a radiant and sublime mental being joining in the nature of the infinite mind of which I for my part and in whom I live and move and have my being I pour out generously on others my best work in efforts my richest thoughts and emotions I give to the world the very best of me the more unselfishly I give the more richly I am blessed the more abundantly our life choices gifts showered on me Your earnest endeavor this GIF showered on me give to the world the best you have not only your labor your work your earnest endeavor but your inspiration the very best that is in you not only work in the usual sense of the word not only labor by accomplishing your daily tasks better than ever before but in addition work mentally and creatively strive to do something fresh create something new add something to the world's total sum of joy and happiness this is accomplished by spending your spare time and concentration in the silence still the outer mind in the senses and then in the Silently listen to the small voice of inspiration then will you receive your message which will send you out into life with the glow of passionate desire in your heart in this way you will conceive that creative ability which until now may have eluded you.

"I AM

Two of the most powerful words,

For what you put after them

Shapes your reality."

CHAPTER 4

UNLOCKING YOURSELF

An unconscious mind is an amazing tool that makes our everyday work so easy. People do not realize that our unconscious mind directs 80% of our bodily actions. There are so many embedded programs inside our unconscious mind that have been taught to us by our parents, Things that we have learned from society and things that we have learned from our friends as we grew up. Our heart is part of our unconscious mind. It continues to beat without us even knowing on a day-to-day basis or consciously thinking that our heart is beating to keep our body and mind alive every day. So some programs have been embedded within our unconscious mind that we consciously ignore that is creating all the problems in our lives today; we may have been embedded with these programs unconsciously by our parents whose programs could have come from their parents. What are programs in our unconscious mind? from the time we are born up to the age of 7, our brains are wired by all the actions and feelings around us. As a child, the many different things that we notice our society and culture doing are deeply embedded inside our free work in our mind that affects us even till today. We have to make a conscious effort to rewire those learnings take them away from our unconscious thinking and rewire them with new learnings that help us achieve our goals in our current life.

I was probably four years old when my first memory serves where I go up to my father and ask him to buy something for me. I don't exactly remember what. He tells me that today is Tuesday and it's a bad day for us to start anything new. It would not give us good luck in our lives. I kept that in my mind and there have been some days where I asked him to buy on Monday. He would tell me that it's almost Tuesday, so we still cannot buy, and the only time we can even look at even going to the stores would be on Wednesday. Now I do not know if my dad was playing with me and just trying to avoid me going to the stores and trying to buy something, or he really meant from his past experiences or what his parents told him that Tuesday was not a good day start anything new. This idea has been stuck in my head, I'm 35 years old today, and I still hesitate to buy something on a Tuesday I would hesitate to sign new deals with customers on Tuesdays, buy clothes or even get a haircut for that matter. But over the years, some of the best deals that have signed have been on Tuesdays, but that I'm conscious part of my brain always kicks in even till today every Tuesday so these are the kind of programs there are embedded in our heads start we need to unlearn I'll put in positive learnings to help us with our day-to-day activities.

If you ask someone what the one main reason they cannot work on themselves is, I'm trying to learn a new skill set; the biggest excuse or reason they are going to give you is that they do not have the time to work on it. Time plays a crucial factor in our life; we have minimal time in the greater meaning of life on this earth. This funny incident happened to me at a gathering when I approached my teacher and said I don't have the time to do this task that was given to me. The teacher smiled and asked me do you know who the president of the country is. I smiled and responded by saying, yes, Sir, I do, The President of our country is Barack Obama. The teacher responded by asking me - if I thought the president was much busier than me and that he would not have the time to work on his skills? And the response I gave was yes. And my teacher, with a sarcastic smile on his, tells him that the difference between the president's busy time and his busy time would be my friend's free time and that would be enough time to work on your skills.

Five ways to rewire our unconscious mind:

1. Positive thoughts: people may think, there are so many people telling us this on social media and platforms, I do not want to hear this again? Well, have we given it a thought as to why so many people are saying this? Every thought that we have has a certain frequency to it and receptors receive that similar frequency. It gets in sync

with other energies that have the same frequency and attracts similar frequencies back to you in the form of people we surround ourselves with or actions.

2. Repeatability: any positive action and thoughts that we undertake to get ourselves to the goals we have must have repeatability. The more positive thoughts we put out, the more come back in. Practice makes perfect.
3. Set your goals and have a visualization board in front of you.
4. Morning Ritual: when you get up each morning, the first 15 mins are most crucial, your in the phase of transition from the unconscious to the conscious and it's the best time to listen to positive affirmations and write down our daily goals and automatically our subconscious will lead us in the direction that will help complete our goals
5. Hypnosis: there has always been a taboo against hypnosis, but it's the most effective way to reprogram the mind. You can listen to the audio while you sleep and have it play in the background and it will act on your subconscious and reprogram it.

"Energy can neither be created nor destroyed but can only be transferred from one form to another"

— First law of Thermodynamics

Chapter 5

CREATING YOUR OPPORTUNITIES

As immigrants coming into the United States, we are bound by certain rules and regulations that have many limitations in us exploring the various avenues of opportunities out there. For example, an international student coming into the country on an F1 visa can work only 20 hours on campus. Once he gets into a full-time job that is 40 hours a week and his or her H1B visa, we are restricted to work in one place.

At work, I was a startup engineer or intern, as the world calls it. The law stated that I was supposed to be paid a certain amount for my Master's degree in engineering. U.S. regulations dictate that we need to be working in the STEM field once we finish our graduation and gives a master's graduate student 27 months internship period. During this period, The company can pay the employee based on the internship position. They could hire a Master's degree student at an hourly wage. I continued to do the work that was given to me. I've been with this company a little over ten years now and I look back at the journey, and it has given me a lot of learning experiences. If I've been with this company for almost ten years, I've done something right and I have been given my due credit at some point in time; otherwise, I wouldn't be here this long. There was a time in the oil and gas industry after the boom in the United States where the entire market crashed towards the latter part of 2014 all the way up to 2016. There were huge job cuts, pay cuts and a lot of companies shut down filing for bankruptcy. During every recession or slowdown in the market, I learned that it is time for us to work even harder and gain more market share. The harder we work during a slow down, the better we come off when things pick back up. Now coming back to my story at my workplace, I started as an engineer like I mentioned above. My life was chugging along and I was this enthusiastic kid wanting to prove something and be useful for the team and try to make progress. I was pretty confident of my skills coming in. Still, even those skills were challenged to an extent where I felt that I hadn't learned anything in all my years of education. Corporate was a new ball game altogether and I was taking baby steps into this world. I changed my mindset. I changed how I did things how to reprogram myself to the changes that the corporate world needed. I did not let the world batter me down. No, if I had let my guard down and took the route that OK, it's recession I'm just an engineer I'm not going to be doing anything I'm not going to be doing any research I just let nature take its course. If I had just warmed the seat back then, I wouldn't have achieved what I achieved I had to break that barrier inside of me to achieve this. I thank my boss and the company for giving me the opportunities to break these barriers at these different points in time and the belief they had in a young guy that he would be able to bring more to the table. I am grateful that I had mentors like my boss in the company that lead an individual.

So Friends' opportunities come and knock on our doors in various forms. We may not know which door to open to find the right opportunity, but for me, what has worked best is to open every door that comes because you never know which door will lead you to the path of greater success.

We should not be limited in our abilities because of a paper that is a visa; we can be stuck in this long line of green card backlogs and just sit and wait and do nothing about it and wait for some politicians and lawmakers to finally come up saying OK I grant you your life are you gonna be sitting around and waiting for things to happen?

"Do not speak badly of yourself, for the Warrior that is inside of you hears your words and is lessened by them."

— David Gemmell

CHAPTER 6

THE WARRIOR WITHIN

Our bodies are in a state of rest when we are sleeping. When it is about time to wake up, our neurons in the brain start firing up; we are In a state of mind where the warrior within ourselves is woken up. The first 15 mins activate the subconscious mind, and during this time, our mind is in the best condition to take in any new programs we want to feed into our brains. We have the power within ourselves to determine how we would like our day to be; if we write down our tasks for the day – we will unconsciously be able to finish all the tasks for the day.

Morning Positive affirmations: We can notice that when we get up in the morning on a day-to-day basis, our conscious mind is at its weakest state and our subconscious mind is at its peak. This is the best time to attract positive affirmations to your mind and the tasks that we need to get done for the day.

There have been days when I would get up and play the news or listen to my favorite song; you may realize that the song or that news is stuck in the head during the entire day. You would use that during the day to converse with friends and family. This is the power of our brain, and our subconscious gets in tune with it. The universe vibrates at a particular frequency and nature is in sync with that frequency. We, as humans, also need to be in sync with nature and its frequency. How do the animals know when to hibernate and come out of hibernation at the exact time? Or how do the trees know that it's time for fall or summer or winter? They know because they are in sync with nature. Human beings need to be in sync with nature; we have come into this world from mother earth and go back into mother earth.

When we are in sync with nature, we will automatically get up at 3:40 AM. Our human system functions in a certain way, so there's been awareness about making use of this possibility; your life is a result of various things that we call the universe, many things that we refer to as existence, so we are a consequence of a certain phenomenal happening that we call his cosmos. We do not exist all by ourselves - we need to be in sync with nature to exist. So when we get in sync, certain things will happen. Human beings have lost sync with nature. We think that is our nature. All the many diseases and problems that human beings are suffering are because we have lost awareness of how to be In sync with the many forces that are making us who we are. If you're conscious, suddenly, a certain spark of aliveness will happen within you. Even if you're in a night of deep sleep, you will come awake. This must happen to you. This means you're falling In sync with life.

How do we attain this? Discipline. When we have Discipline in our lives, we will be able to achieve great things. What are the simple things in life that we can do to attain this Discipline and awaken this inner warrior within us?

a.   Being Grateful for everything that we have in our lives. A simple prayer thanking the universe and writing down the things that we have been grateful for. Embrace the haves and stop worrying about the have nots in the world.

b.   Forgive; when we forgive and let go, and it gives us a sense of calm. Our minds work better. Holding all that fear and negative emotions creates negative energy. When we have that negative field around us, we repeatedly attract more of the same energy. By letting off all the negativity, we catapult ourselves ahead

c.   Meditation: sitting down, closing your eyes and feeling the heat beat – envision a light traveling inside your heart. The calmness and slow breathing will take you into your personal space and make your mind connect with the universe. It has been a great strength for me to tune into my senses. You will be amazed as to how the energy changes. Suddenly, you will start realizing that there are simple solutions to the most complex problems as we get in sync with our body, mind, and soul.

d.   Eating healthy: I enjoy being a vegetarian and it has been 11 years since I have converted from being a non-vegetarian, It's a new year resolution that has stuck, but here I am a decade later,

I feel like a much better person. As Sadhguru says, what we eat becomes a part of us; we imbibe the characteristics and emotions of what we eat. Being a vegetarian has made me less aggressive and do not get angry. Eating the right balance of food for the body affects the neurochemical makeup of the brain. It has a large effect on the mind-body connection.

e. Sleep and exercise: Line any machine in the world; our body needs proper maintenance. It needs adequate sleep for it to kickback in the morning and rejuvenates. And more important is the exercise that we do. The various chemicals that are secreted during these activities reduce stress levels and anxiety, and this leads to better energy levels

There are three straightforward actions we can master daily, and this applies to every work or chore that we do...

a. Finish what you begin

b. Do it a little bit more than you can

c. Do it better than you think you can

"If you correct your mind, the rest will fall into place."

— Lao Tsu

CHAPTER 7

YOUR THOUGHTS CREATES YOUR LIFE

The Power Of Positive thinking

I just applied for my extension for my H1B visa. I was very skeptical about the extension's results. I was worried and always thinking about the negative aspects of the visa getting rejected. I was thinking so negatively that it consumed my day-to-day activities. These thoughts were running in my head when I wake up in the morning, when I am at work, and when I come home. I was overthinking about the extensions; now, what made me get to that stage was the coronavirus situation. The government had made several changes to the immigrant visa programs, which kept bugging me a lot. And I know that this is just not me it's a lot of people out there who are being affected by this, and my sympathies go out to every one of them, but we should understand the core of the problem is our mindset. I was worried because the elections were coming. I did not know who would come into power and what changes they will bring to the immigration laws. It's going to bring a lot of uncertainty with the green card bill in play. No, my work request for me to travel and I'll have to go to India for me to do the stamping and now with no international flights and travel restrictions all over the world and the council it's being shut down due to the virus, the challenge is for us to even travel to our homelands for us to stamp our passports, and this was a bigger concern why are we being held captives here an always focusing on the negative side. Why should we not be worried about the visas because these are beyond our control, and it is best left to the lawmakers and the country's politicians to make the best decisions? And we should do what is right and what is correct in the given spectrum of the loss that has been established, but what does this do in terms of us overthinking and being worried and bogged down soul what the outcome is going to be. John has been mentoring me for close to 8 years now. I have reached out to him on various occasions in my life, and he has advised me during different stages. He has always emphasized the power of positive thinking. So I decide to put this into action find had advised that think about you getting the approval notice, stay in that moment for some time, rejoice in the moment then come back to your normal. This activates certain functions of your brain where you're trying to rewire negative thinking in positive thinking. I continued to do this on a day to day basis, to my own surprise, I see that I'm no longer worried about the visa outcome. I'm happy, I'm content and it does not affect my work. I totally forgot that I applied for my extension and was just going about my day-to-day work my attention was not on it at all. I was focusing my energy at work and trying to bring more business during these trying times.

About a month passed I totally forgot about the extension that used to pop up in my head randomly but did not make a great impact; I just knew that it was out there and I used to forget it immediately. Three months go by, and I was like, hey, I think it's about time. I need to check what my application's status was, and when I checked, I see that it had been approved almost a month ago. I was a little bit relieved I was not over ecstatic because I kept visualizing this moment over and over again every day and I relive that moment every single time when it actually happened. I knew I had done something right and positive thinking.

CHAPTER 8

HEARTFULNESS - DISCOVERING YOURSELF

A naïve young teenager out of college, looking into the world of possibilities – I was following the age-old tradition of the societal values I have been programmed with. I have been introduced to Meditation's life through transcendental Meditation, where we were asked to recite a mantra in our head. As a young kid of 14-15 did not make much of an impact, and I thought it was for people of my parent's age and that I had a long winding way ahead for me to get to do this. My belief has always been to do good and help as many people in your life and karma will do good. I have never been someone who believed in idol worship and the austerities that went along with it. Life was OK for me, and then my mom and her sisters joined a new meditation course called Sahaj marg.

I used to drop my mother regularly at the ashram on Sundays. I return home one day from college, and there is a lot of hush-hush at the house. My dad had a nervous smile on his face when he met me and my grandmother was telling my dad not to worry and that it will all be well. During the evening, I realized that my mom had gone in for a regular medical check-up at the hospital. I heard a few conversations where the word medical reports were being mentioned. It did not signal any alarm to me as my mother and grandmother were both medical doctors by profession. These medical terminologies were common in my household. My ears perked when I heard my grandmother tell my dad that he let mom go in for another check-up and that is when I asked her what had happened. The initial medical reports reported a cyst-like growth near the spleen and a possibility of it being cancerous. The seriousness of the issue hit me then.

I noticed that my mother would spend a lot of time in the meditation room – 10 years later, when I was 25, she told me what exactly happened. 2 reports confirming that it was a cancerous cyst (excuse me for not using the right terminology) – she told me that she in her day to day routine for a period completely handed over the children's and husbands life to "Master" who in Sahaj marg is the teacher (guru). So intense was her belief in this system and the Master that she had immersed herself in this completely. She described what could have been only a miracle – mummy said during the meditation one day she felt uneasy. Something odd happened and then suddenly felt as if something had been pulled out of her body. She came back into consciousness from the trance state. She did not put much thought into that.

A few days later, during a follow-up with the doctor on her scan and reports, the doctors said that the cyst-like substance was just fat showing on the scan reports. All she needed was some exercise to burn that fat. This was a complete 180 from what was first diagnosed. I never believed in miracles, and I was gobsmacked when she told me this story. I was surprised for two reasons: firstly, I was not aware that something this serious was going on in our lives. I was not privy to it and second that a miracle had happened. I am someone who has never believed in these kinds of miracles when people talk on the television. I have always felt these to be orchestrated and money-making scams. But why would my mom lie to me? What does she stand to gain? I thought. A realization smacked my head hard that day – BELIEF and a newfound respect for the system Sahaj marg.

I got interested In Meditation and wanted to experience this. She told me that I had to sit with a preceptor and take three sittings before starting the practice. I was all excited and when for me first sitting with this elderly gentleman in his mid-sixties maybe. He tells me about the practice and what needs to be done. In my mind, this was so simple – all he told me was to think about light in my heart, and I questioned why I needed to that. He just said that it was our way of thanking our heart for being there for yes 24/7. I said OK, and then he said do not control your thoughts and that when you realize that you have wandered, come back to concentrating on your heart.

I was happy that it was simple and I could get done with this quickly and he asked me to close my eyes and start Meditation.

Here and there, I was returning my thoughts to heart, and I did not realize that 30 mins had passed so quickly and he said, "that's all" I opened my eyes as if I was woken up from a trance and my mind was calm. The preceptor looks at me and explains certain energies and thoughts and how I needed to direct those thoughts. Part of me was scared that I did not want to come back the next day to do my second sitting. How in the world did this person figure out my thoughts? Was I hallucinating? I left the place with a very nostalgic feeling. The next two sittings had minimal conversations, and I kept it just the Meditation and instructions. I was relieved that the sittings were done and that I could start the practice now.

I was thinking about my heart more now after the jolt that this preceptor gave me. That day I realized that there was something more in this world than just our daily routines in life, which needs to be felt and not explained.

I started to dig deeper into this practice, and I was amazed that people came in huge numbers. I tell myself that there must be something in this. If not, why would there be such a big following? I started to see a change in the mother's general behavior – she was stress-free. I started getting quite inquisitive and started my practice.

It would start with a 30-minute meditation in the morning – just to close my eyes and meditate, thinking that there is a light in your heart. My breathing starts to get really low. I was advised to maintain a diary where I should write down everything I felt like writing down, be it problems, solutions, concerns etc..there was another part of this Meditation that interested me was the past life "impressions". The teachings believe certain impressions that have been created in our past life has led us to the now and where we are and make us experience the current learning we are going through. Every day of our lives, we witness and see various things that cause impressions in our minds and sit down for a cleansing process in the evening. This is just me sitting down and thinking about the day's events and picturizing the events of the day, the thoughts leaving our body through the tail bone of our body – this removes the impressions for the day. We are now tackling the impressions for the day; now, what about our past lives? What the system suggests is that we go to a preceptor once a week for the sitting and they help with past-life impressions. The feeling explained to me by one of the aunts is like taking a firewater hose and directing all the pressure and energy on you to remove all the dirt (impressions) from you. This would remove our past life impressions and helps us progress towards self-realization.

One day on a Saturday, I was bored and thought, let me read all the writings I have made in this diary after the meditation and cleansing process every day – to my surprise I saw that I had given solutions to my own problems and in a way had solved the posed question. It was a state déjà vu feeling for me when I read this. I wondered as to how this could be possible? It dawned on me that we are the creators of our own problems and our determination to solve a problem but our thought process in the right direction. Once our thought process changes, our actions change.

If we fill positivity in our mind, it can only give out positivity. It's like a computer – data in, data out. What you feed the computer is what output it gives. If you put a virus in it – it gives out a bad experience. This is tied to the concept of shadows that we have discussed in the earlier chapter. Every day we are put in situations from which we are destined to get a learning. Once we spiritually gather this learning we were, we have the power of our thoughts to ensure we do not see negative learning come by again.

The systems also have what they call whispers from the brighter world where the Masters have sent messages, and one such message opened my mind up.

"In physics, the core is the central part of an atom, made up of protons and neutrons. There is a vacuum in its center, known for centuries by mystics and finally detected by scientists, who haven't really identified it – which is the core of divine energy" – whispers from the brighter world, Sahaj Marg.

Akashic records

We are fortunate to live in an awakened and conscious living era, where any information can be received instantly. In an age of exploring the purposes of life and ways of helping others and in turn ourselves. One of the universe's gifts to guide us into our inner self or self-actualization is the akashic record.

The usual way of approaching any problem is by ignoring the problem or trying to do so. Ignoring one's problems would only help in worsening the situation since we lack clarity on the problem itself.

Secondly, one would try to approach a problem to solve it. This usually is brought about by reading books on personal development or seeking assistance from others; this would not help solve the problem at the root level.

One can solve any type of problem by accepting the problem as is. Though this would be difficult at the start, once a person is open to accept the problem, one tends to understand the root cause; this helps us find a solution to the so-called problem. Therefore, the negative position is transformed into an opportunity for growth.

Understanding why such problems occur and accepting them provides us with learning and growth opportunities; it helps us tap into our Akashic records.

The akashic records, which are also known as the book of life our the God's book of Remembrance or the cosmic mind or the universal mind or the eye of God; the akashic records are made up of the energy of everything in the universe, and this energy is known as the energy of love. Akasha means AKA meaning "storage place," and SHA meaning "hidden," which overall means "unseen storage space or an unseen space."

To simplify, it is a supercomputer system of the universe; just like how cloud computing works today, it's a central server where every person who has ever lived has information. It consists of an individual's thoughts, feelings, intents, deeds, etc., from all their lifeforms from the source until it returns to the source. It has a tremendous impact on our relationships, feelings, beliefs, our potentials, and our everyday life as well.

The akashic records are the record of one's soul's journey from the source until you return. This energy not only holds all our thoughts, feelings and actions from each lifetime but is interconnected to everyone and everything around us.

Each individual has their own Masters or beings of light, also called guidance Angels, to help one throughout their lifetime. By tapping into this energy field, one can seek guidance from them to complete our purpose in this lifetime. We can also fulfill any past vows, eliminate bad karma, build good karma, support people belonging to our soul family, etc. We can also tap into this energy field to help us answer any negative blocks or obstructions in our current life form and help us overcome any emotional pain, mental or health blocks, and guide us into the right path of life.

Do the meaning of akashic record is hidden storage space. It can be easily accessed by anyone anytime. As a matter of fact, everyone has unknowingly accessed these records an ample number of times. Do you remember when you had any hunch, gut feeling, or a flash of intuition, all these are glimpses from your akashic records.

The akashic records can be easily accessed through prayer meditation and intuition. An individual can gain access by intentionally opening their intuition; this is the best way to gain access to the akashic records by providing the universe with the loving energy as the records themselves.

"Wherever you go, go with all your heart" – Confucius.

Chapter 9

The View

People underestimate the power of the heart. The majority of the people realize that a heart is beating only when they realize a certain emotion within them, be it pain, happiness, sadness, sorrow, exuberating, etc. Little do we realize that the heart continues to pump non stop 24/7 until our last breath. The heart's size is only as big as the palm; when you ask someone which side is the heart? They may point towards the left or the right. Our heart, my friend, is bang in the exact center. It is your powerhouse and it is your lifeline; time is short, and the opportunity out there is very great. Invaluable goals, it is a price that is worth any sacrifice of time and effort. As Chariji says, this body is but the soul's vehicle to take us from birth into eternity, which we call liberation.

There have been many instances where I have been heartbroken and completely shattered. The problems that we go through sometimes completely under the wraps of people around us who suffer "lonely." Still, at every moment, my heart was with me and guiding me. I was a fool on multiple occasions when I felt a huge weight on my heart, and I used to assume that as heartburn and I used to ignore it. Little did I know that it was trying to talk to me and giving me a solution. I needed to have the mindset to listen to my heart, which I did not have at an earlier age.

I can sing praises about spirituality and guide you to spiritual teachers – it may come out as false praise and con man acts. Still, you will encounter your heart, and it will always tell you what is right and wrong. Once your mind is made up to seek that light in your heart, it will automatically guide you in the right direction to seek your path. Once the seed is sown, it is irreversible – it all depends on how we water it and care for it. Without you consciously thinking about it, the tree of spirituality is growing within you.

In the current scenario, everyone is always worried about the political and economic scenario, coronavirus, unemployment, environmental hazards, and immigration. The waiting lines are long and tedious; we must learn to enjoy the wait, however hard the road ahead seems. Let's not forget that we need to live our present and enjoy the moment rather worry about the wait in the line and worry about what the future holds and spoil our present- you have heard this saying a million times. Still, have we really sat down for a minute to reflect on this and realize how true all of this really is?

What does your heart say to you when you sit down and ask what the problem really is waiting in this long line? We only hear these high verbatim words such as security, freedom, family, and status – really? Does this feel that moving ahead in the line and achieving this goal will give you all of this? Nope, it is not going to provide you with that.

Let's do a small exercise; I would like for you all to sit down in a relaxed posture and close your eyes and meditate on your heart for 2 minutes. Once you feel relaxed and in the zone- think about the event that has been worrying you the most and you have been wanting or waiting for the most. Imagine that the event has been successfully achieved and go ahead 15 mins. You feel happy, you have a sense of relief, you feel on top of the world, you want to share that information with all of your well-wishers, and while you are in this state, you would feel that all this time I was worried, I ignored my job, I neglected my family and kids, my parents and my own life – it was such a waste of time and energy. This is the simple "view," my friends; always visualize it in a positive direction.

Our thoughts are our actions; we classify a thought as a positive thought or a negative thought when we think in our head. We should understand why our mind is classifying these thoughts as such? Just us thinking that this thought is bad or good has no power to that thought. It is only when those thoughts start making you do things unconsciously that they negatively affect it. Now how do we classify these thoughts as good or bad? It's based on the information fed into the mind; when we start associating ourselves with things that we are not internally, it causes us negative unconscious actions. So we need to make a conscious effort to what feed that goes into our mind, be it visual or mental; we absorb those things into the mind, and when we try to become something, we are not based on those feeds that our unconscious actions kick in that is where we struggle with our thought process and mindset. Just like a computer, "data in" "data out," and in the process, our action is the "view" we portray.

There is this famous story where an artist goes to a King who admired art a lot and puts forward his wish to paint something spectacular for his majesty and requests the king for a blank wall to show off his potential. In the same room stood another man who requests the king for the same thing but puts forth something interesting. He tells the king that he can paint the same thing the other painter is painting without looking at what he is drawing. At first, the King, skeptical, grants his wish and instructs that a huge curtain be drawn between the two walls. Here is the first painter armed with all his paints and brush sets to work on his painting; interestingly, the other was only armed with a cloth and water. Days turn into weeks and weeks into months. Finally, the painting was done; the artist invites the king to see his work. The king looks at the painting and is completely mesmerized and rewards the painter with a huge sum. He turns to the other man who claimed he could replicate the painting and asks him if his painting was done and he said yes. The king orders the curtains to be pulled down and, to his astonishment, sees the same replica – every color, every curve, and every line the same. The king exuberant awards this man much bigger and asks him how he does it, to which the man responds, "Your majesty, all I did was to polish the marble every day to make it shine like a mirror and reflected the other artist's painting."

All our problems and worries are a part of our mind's chatter and our thought process. Just like the marble wall, our minds need to be polished every day, and that's the hard work that needs to be done in the process of bringing out all the hidden actions and thoughts that have been buried. The best way to avoid chatter in mind is to "NEGLECT IT," surround yourself with positive news, positive people, and their energy with reflecting of your polished mirror-like mind.

"What lies behind you and what lies in front of you, pales in comparison to what lies inside of you" – Ralph Waldo Emerson.

Printed in Great Britain
by Amazon